The Burren WALL

by Gordon D'Arcy

First published in 2006 by Tír Eolas,
Newtownlynch, Kinvara, Co. Galway.

Text, photos and illustrations
© Gordon D'Arcy except drawings
page 25, 31, 34-36 © Anne Korff.

ISBN 1 873821 16 6
ISBN 9 781873 821169

British Library Cataloguing in
Publication Data.
A catalogue record for this book is
available from the British Library.

All rights reserved. No part of this
publication may be reproduced,
copied or transmitted in any form
without the written permission of
the publisher.

Cover and layout: Anne Korff and
Johan Hofsteenge.
Typesetting: Johan Hofsteenge.
Printed in Ireland by Betaprint.

This publication has received support
from the Heritage Council under the
2006 Publications Grant Scheme.

CONTENTS

Introduction	4
The Burren wall through history	9
The drystone wall. A work of skill, a work of art.	25
Visitors' views	33
Britain's Burren – the Yorkshire Dales	37
The Natural History of the Burren wall	41
Bibliography	61

INTRODUCTION

One of the most notable features of the Burren is the wall – the 'drystone' wall. It is a remarkable feature throughout Ireland. More than half a million kilometres exist but in the open landscape of the Burren it is integral and its visual impact is so powerful as to be compelling. Locals living with these walls day to day pass no remark but visitors are invariably fascinated. The apparent haphazardness of their layout and fragility of construction are consistent subjects of inquiry for those whose landscapes are more formally or securely bounded. In the absence of high vegetation and other obscuring features, the eye is drawn to the stone walls and inclined to follow their distinctive longitudinal and criss-cross pattern across the landscape, gaining some sense of scale in the process. The Burren's habitats – open limestone pavement, terraced hillsides, upland plateau, coastal flatlands, even the temporary wetlands, turloughs – appear stitched together by lines of walls. Their image remains in one's consciousness, even after departing the region.

This superficial network has evocations of a subterranean counterpart – the labyrinth of caverns and underground systems – often unseen by the visitor. As with the dolmen, the gentian, or the cave, the drystone wall is a motif for the Burren. Who built these walls? When? Why were so many built in such stark circumstances? In attempting to

Light through drystone wall, Pullagh

Typical Aran Island wall, Inis Oirr

Medieval field boundary, Fahee South

satisfy these and other queries, answers tend to be elusive, as in most Burren topics; mystery inevitably remains. The wall might reasonably be defined as a land boundary. But who would go to so much trouble in such poor land, for so little apparent gain? As in so many Burren enigmas the issue is complex. For instance, the long-term change wrought on the Burren, resulting in the eroded and overgrazed landscape familiar today, is a product both of human endeavour and the elements. Which has been the more significant is difficult to say for the natural process of limestone solution has obliterated the evidence.

Archaeological investigation, however, has shown that clearing and enclosing the land for livestock and crops has been going on for as long as people have sought to survive in this stony region. Was the wall originally intended as an enclosure or an exclosure? Perhaps both? The distinction is important in the context of the development of husbandry: containing crops and livestock is an agricultural fundamental; keeping out predators – both animal and human – is as old as farming itself.

Cross walls, goat and cattle shelters, sheep passes, booley huts, and so on are local farming architectural features that punctuate the Burren uplands, testimony to the versatility of the raw material and the ingenuity of generations of 'mountainy' men. The Burren wall, in its many forms, has rightly been described as a monument to the farmer.

Walls are also clearance, stock-piles. Strewn stones that might otherwise injure beasts or interfere with planting are handily consigned to the boundaries, perhaps for future reuse. Could the availability of stone have been a factor in determining the size of the fields: more stone; smaller enclosures? Stones gathered thus or quarried from adjacent outcrops have buttressed many a rampart. Conversely, Burren monuments have been disassembled and reused in wall construction down the ages; most vulnerable have been the prehistoric cairns with their handy-sized stones. But even the massive orthostats of wedge tombs have occasionally been incorporated into Burren walls.

The style of construction of the wall has provided us with an aesthetic form, as in country crafts, generally, that has its roots in practicality: the wall as a functional work of art. Inherent knowledge of how best to build, to withstand storms, has dictated the manner in which stones are chosen, laid and the wall intermittently strengthened. Maximum endurance using a minimum of material is facilitated by the limestone's high frictional characteristics. Not that the builders were imbued with scientific insight: a case of intuition rather than tuition; right-brain rather than left.

On the Aran Islands, geologically if not politically part of the Burren, the drystone wall attains its finest expression, its layered strength and style echoed in the weave of the Aran sweater. In Tim Robinson's estimation there are more than two thousand km of stone walls, in total, on the Aran Islands. The single wall, one stone deep, is the classic 'minimalist' style of construction but double walls, two stones thick with a 'rubble' core are also common, particularly on better agricultural land. *Feidín* walls, constructed with base courses of small stones, are a feature of land that once was arable, the small stones having been cleared for ploughing. These are commonest on thicker soils. Other nuances of style may be found where local conditions or extraneous influences have impacted.

The Burren wall has been identified as a reliable historical indicator. The earliest 'mound' walls have been approximately dated to the arrival of the first settlers. Slab and tumble walls relate to later periods of settlement and clearance. Plunkett-Dillon (1983) was exercised by the Burren's earliest walls, and recognized them as an indicator of land-use continuity, thus emphasising the uniqueness of the region. Despite episodes of radical land clearance under EU grant-assisted schemes since the 1980s, the Burren retains significant fragments of prehistoric and medieval landscapes to this day. Land, radically modified by modern machinery, is characteristically bounded by megalith-sized stones. Heaped up by the bucket of the JCB, these walls, as with their early counterparts, will doubtless one day be identifiable as to their period of construction. Between these ancient and modern chronological abutments lie six thousand years of design, each settlement period reflecting the aspirations, fears, physical capability and technological advances of its people.

Links with others living in similar circumstances elsewhere in the world have shown the universality of the stone wall. Cumbria's karst region, though geographically and culturally separate from the Burren, shows a similar commitment to the drystone wall. Consistency in design reflects commonality in stone-lore and need. However, livestock preference (sheep rather than cattle) has dictated obvious differences. Research has shown that 19th century Irish emigrants – perhaps from Clare – built miles of stone walls in Kentucky to consistent and recognisable styles. Similar evidence, legacy of the diaspora, is emerging from other countries besides. What other parts of the world retain, unknown, such tangible examples of our early wall-builders?

The new millennium has seen increased urbanisation of the west of Ireland. Where stone walls once defined agricultural land, they now bound large gardens and straightened roads. In general (with the judicious use of concrete) they have become more decorative than functional. The stone-faced, concrete-block core echoes the 'cosmetic' thatch with its fireproof underlay. Aesthetics, though no longer the unselfconscious byproduct of craft, remains important: people still hanker after the local and the natural.

Also considered here is another little-appreciated aspect of the Burren wall's heritage: its natural history. Though a human construct, the wall supports interesting and diverse flora and fauna. From the stone itself with its myriad fossils to its inhabiting plants and animals, it is a vital refuge for hundreds of species. It also provides a precious shelterbelt and linear corridor for the distribution of wildlife.

Drystone wall, Moneen Mountain

Garden snail cluster on limestone wall

THE BURREN WALL THROUGH HISTORY

A region's social history, the recorded life and death traditions of its inhabitants, is inscribed initially on the landscape. In Ireland, the remains of former dwelling places such as forts, castles, ruined houses and the repositories of the deceased – megalithic tombs, graveyards, killeens – are familiar loci of inquiry. Stone walls would not normally be regarded as productive, primary sources: in the Burren, however, they are. In this highly modified landscape where social change has left its mark in many forms, the walls speak independently of land clearance, agricultural change, population fluctuation and political transformation. They stand as testimony to the labour of innumerable generations, carrying forward both tried and trusted skills and the innovations of predecessors. Despite an increasing dependence on machinery, block and mortar, little radical change is found in the finished product. The same simple methods used in hand-building stone walls in prehistoric times are still used today. Notwithstanding this, certain features evident in the Burren's walls today can be attributed to particular periods of construction. Research has shown that at least four different wall types are chronologically identifiable.

Prehistoric walls

The original houses of the Burren's first farmers have left little or no trace, but several km of early field boundaries covering about 250 ha are preserved beneath the thin turf on the southern uplands. These **mound** walls, so called because of their appearance as linear, soil-covered mounds, are easily overlooked at ground level. Aerial photography and selective excavation have revealed their true character, showing them to be more widespread than thought at first. Traces of mound wall networks have been detected elsewhere, at Poulnabrone, for instance, and in the vicinity of other megalithic tombs. It is likely that they will eventually be found widely in the Burren. Most of these walls are thought to date from the chronological boundary between the late Neolithic and the early Bronze Age, around 4,400 years ago at a time when the upland farming was expanding in response to a growing population. Much has been written about the layout of mound walls, echoing the comprehensive investigations carried out in the more extensive and older (ca 5,500 year old) Neolithic site at Céide in north Mayo. Professor Caulfield's interpretation

Mound wall, Parknabinnia

Walls, Burren uplands

was that the walls were built primarily as pasture paddocks, to enclose herds of livestock. Although cultivation ridges were found, arable agriculture was thought to be entirely subordinate to husbandry. The Mayo fields generally were rectangular enclosures of up to several hectares, as large as many similar fields today. Those in the Burren are much smaller, ranging from about 0.5 ha (irregular fields) to 2 ha (regular fields). Were the Burren walls used in the same fashion as those at Céide or was there some, now obscure reason for the size difference? Was it simply a case of smaller population and lesser demands? In general, the mound wall network at Roughan Hill in the Burren bears no resemblance to the network of modern walls in the area. It is tempting to conclude that the prehistoric farms were long abandoned before their historic counterparts were established. It has been suggested, given the present structureless form of the collapsed walls at Céide, that they may have been linear clearance piles rather than walls *per se,* that the meagre stones could not have been used to construct viable cattle-containing enclosures. While this might apply at least partially, in the Burren, where abundance of stone in the ground might necessitate such enclosures, it is difficult to see mere stone removal resulting in the neat rectilinear network as at Céide.

The lie of the collapsed walls, allowing for imaginative reconstruction, indicate a similar simple style of construction in both places, though comparison and inference might be misleading, given their antiquity.

Prehistoric enclosure from the air; Oughtmama, Turlough Hill

Those in Mayo, their stones presumably preserved entirely beneath the blanket bog, seem strangely insubstantial given their function as cattle enclosures. They are also without foundations. The Burren mound walls, while not having been sealed in time and having been subject to stone 'recycling', have, in most cases, a limestone pedestal beneath them. This pedestal, a few cm higher than the surrounding land, exists as a consequence of differential erosion, the stones protecting it from the elements. Mound walls were also clearly constructed without foundations. The width of the pedestal – of the order of a metre – may point to a wide-based, tapering cross-section. However, since they have been in a collapsed state for millennia, it could be that the structureless pile of a collapsed single wall would create the same effect.

Rampart wall base; prehistoric enclosure, Turlough Hill

Despite the investigative work to date, the Burren's mound walls still harbour secrets about how they were built and who built them.

Turlough Hill, on the Burren's north uplands, has a remarkable four-hectare enclosure. It is thought to be either a Neolithic/Bronze Age 'Causewayed enclosure' similar to counterparts in Britain, or a Bronze Age/Iron Age Hillfort typical of many upland areas in Ireland. Hopefully, archaeological excavation will help clarify this and indicate something of the monument's former occupiers. The wall, up to three metres wide at the base, may have been formerly also that high. Whether from the adjacent lowlands or from the plateau itself, the visual impact must have been highly dramatic. Nowadays, as a consequence of recycling of stone, the monument is a mere vestige of the original, more clearly defined from the air than from the ground. Despite this, it is still possible to make out the dozen or so entrance/exits where substantial slabs have been put up on their edges to contain the rampart base. In more than one sense, this was no ordinary wall: the enclosure within may have been used as a ritual site or for seasonal gatherings. The scale and mode of construction is a testament to the stone-working skills of the Burren's prehistoric inhabitants.

No greater manifestation of this skill exists than in the wonderful stone forts of the Burren and the Aran Islands. All three islands have stone forts, dating from the first millennium BC; the most magnificent, Dún Dúchathair and Dún Aengus are found on Inis Mór (Árainn). Allowing that both these forts have been somewhat restored and that they may not now look precisely as when they were built, one cannot help but be impressed by the workmanship. It is clear, from the regular shape of the limestone blocks used, that the stone was quarried rather than gathered from the

Prehistoric ramparts; Dún Dúchathair, Árainn

Early Medieval walls

Despite the well-documented Iron Age enigma (political upheaval, farmland abandonment, reinvasion by woodland?), agriculture undoubtedly continued, albeit at a lesser pace than formerly. Our knowledge of the period is limited, to say the least. Did the irregular wall layout that was prevalent in the mound walls continue or did new methods come on stream, reflecting perhaps new developments? The wall builders tell us nothing until the beginning of the great phase of ringfort building in the first millennium AD. The Burren perhaps has more early

Chevaux de frise, *Ballykinvarga*

Medieval field systems, *Ballyelly*

stony hinterland. The elaborate terracing has spawned speculation as to the purpose of these promontory structures. Was their function defensive or ritual, or were they simply examples of prehistoric ostentation? Both forts have a wide apron of upright stones, beyond their ramparts, indicating defence rather than style. Such *chevaux de frise* also surround Ballykinvarga, near Kilfenora in the Burren. Can we therefore date this, the grandest of the Burren's many cahers, also to the Iron Age? In the absence of excavation we can but speculate, but a wander through the elaborate defences into the stronghold of the enclosure evokes both the heroism and hostility synonymous with the 'saga period' prior to the advent of Christianity.

medieval field boundaries than elsewhere in Ireland. An entire central belt of unreclaimed land, from Ailwee in the north to Fanygalvan, and Ballyganner in the south, with extensive offshoots such as the Caher valley and Faunarooska in the west – hundreds of hectares of landscape – remains essentially as it was perhaps a thousand years ago. Stony and agriculturally unpromising, these tracts of land are characterised by a maze of small irregular fields usually associated with stone ringforts (cahers or cashels), the former homes of substantial cattle farmers. One of the best preserved, due to its well-integrated drystone ramparts, is Caherconnell not far from Poulnabrone dolmen. The irregular wall layout associated with these forts is a reflection of the continuing fidelity of the Gaelic farmers to pastoral agriculture: crops continued to be relatively unimportant. Brehon Law such as *Bretha Comaithchesa* (Laws of Neighbourhood) tells us much about the social circumstances of these landowners, of their relationship with their overlords, peers and slaves, and of the crafts and craftspeople in their service. Although there are no diagrams, we know about the various forms of permanent and temporary enclosure. We also learn of the name (*corae*) and dimensions of a stone-built wall. A 'three-stone wall, three feet thick and twelve fists (four feet) high', presumably a structurally stable wall of three courses, perhaps with a rubble centre, is specified. Under Brehon Law also, the wall must be two feet thick half way up and one foot thick at the top. The dimensions suggest a double (base course) to single

Cathair Scríbín from the air, Leamaneh

(top) construction using big stones: it is difficult to find Burren walls answering, even vaguely, to this description today. It is doubtful, therefore, whether 'classical' *corae* were constructed in the Burren in this period. Most of the medieval walls seem to have been erected to a formula based more on experience and expediency than on legal dictate. Many early references in the Laws of Neighbourhood are to semi-permanent or temporary enclosures, which are also clearly specified. The majority were of wattlework and timber rather than of stone. These, of course, have disappeared without trace from the landscape and may never have figured prominently in the Burren.

The wall type specifically identified with the ringfort phase in the Burren, is the **slab wall**. This style of wall is quite prevalent: large limestone flags set up on edge, perhaps overlapped and infilled with smaller material or used in conjunction with brushwood or felled timber. Aerial photography shows them as enclosing small irregular fields around many of the forts where the land has not been recently reclaimed. Judging from the abundance of the remains of such walls, it seems that their widespread use was a natural response to local conditions. Presumably such use was not confined to the early medieval period.
They must have been made as availability and conditions demanded; limestone slabs set up against one another in the fashion of the medieval walls may be found in an entirely modern context in one or two places. Good examples of the 'real thing' can be seen near the road at Fahy south, near Carron, and surrounding the ninth century cliff-fort of Cahercommaun. Research indicates that slab walls typically enclose areas ranging from 0.2 ha to 6 ha. There are other places, such as in the enclosed valley behind Ailwee hill, where many hectares of medieval fields are enclosed by collapsed stone walls which differ little from those still being constructed by hand in the Burren today. These **tumble walls**, as they are known, have been shown by Plunkett-Dillon to be widespread, often being associated with stone ringforts, enclosing small strip-shaped or block-shaped regular and small irregular fields. In her estimate, the field size was always small, less than 1.6 ha.

Slab wall, Parknabinnia

Medieval tumble walls, Gleninsheen

workmanship. This triad of skills is clearly visible also in the region's many ecclesiastical structures – from the simplicity of St Gobnet's tiny oratory on Inis Oirr to the grandeur of Corcomroe Abbey. Though much of the stone used in ecclesiastical building was quarried and cut for the specific buildings, adaptation of existing structures and recycling of material is also evident. Incorporated into the wall of the ruined 13th century Carron church is the cut stone of an earlier window.

Inside a souterrain, Ballinastaig ringfort, South Galway

Barony wall, East Burren uplands

Despite their collapsed state, it has been deduced that tumble walls originally were single walls (a single line of stones, one on top of the other). In addition, where tumble walls intersected with modern single walls, there is invariably a gap in the tumble wall, indicating that the stones of the former were used in constructing the latter. Further evidence of the skills of Gaelic stone wall builders (if any were needed) is manifest in the souterrain (*uaimh thalún*), the underground tunnel beneath many ringforts. Souterrains were constructed as parallel drystone walls lining either side of a deep ditch. Massive stone slabs laid on top sealed the tunnel, save for a trap-door entrance within the fort. Their solidity over a span of more than a thousand years demonstrates not only impressive organisation but also cleverness in design and superb

Medieval walls

It has been stated that no substantial redevelopment of field boundaries occurred throughout the latter Gaelic period, that apart from normal kin-inheritance subdivision, the medieval field network remained largely unaltered throughout. Tangible evidence relating to the redefining of clan boundaries appears to be wanting. The townland boundaries, for instance, are frequently co-terminus with farms, having formerly coincided with Gaelic land divisions. Presumably the *tuaths* of the O'Loughins and the O'Connors – the major Gaelic landowners of the region in medieval times – were marked by clearly defined boundaries, originally prominent topographical features, latterly strongly-built stone walls. It would seem reasonable to conclude that the present-day barony boundaries correspond to the earlier Gaelic subdivisions. The long wall running along the eastern escarpment from Corranroo to the foot of Slieve Carran may be an example.

Despite the powerful evidence of the thirty or so ruined castles or towerhouses, we know little about the impact of their builders on the wall layout. Since it is difficult to ascribe particular systems of walls to the Gaelic nobility, it has been suggested that they simply continued with the farms and settlement boundaries of earlier times, moving from cashel to castle in the period from the 15th to the 17th century, when most of the towerhouses were constructed. The fact that several of the towerhouses were actually constructed within cashels tends to bear this out. In contrast to the rather formulaic design of the keeps, the strongly-built rectilinear bawns enclosing them show amazing variation. No doubt much of this is due to recycling. The stylish crenellate bawn at Muckinish, for instance, is clearly a relatively modern construct: a piece of the lower unmortared original remains on the seaward side. But what of the 'megalithic' enclosure at Ballinalacken? Is this the immoveable base course of the former bawn or some unfinished modern substitute?

17th century estate wall, Leamaneh castle

The Gaelic order appears to have continued in the Burren well into the latter 17th century, long after it had died out elsewhere in Ireland. The Brehon Laws, for instance, were still being taught at the O'Daveron law school at Cahermacnachtan at this time. An example of late Gaelic construction is to be seen in the curtilage of Leamaneh castle. A rectilinear wall up to three metres high and stoutly built at the base encloses the original deer park. Much of this wall, built presumably by Conor O'Brien in the first half of the 17th century to contain his herd of fallow deer, is still in fair standing today. Well-constructed, lime-mortared cylindrical turrets at the corners were probably more decorative than functional. It has been deduced from maps of the O'Brien estate that many of the large, irregular fields were built between 1640 and the middle of the 18th century. This probably represents the shift from subsistence agriculture to a market economy, following the establishment of effective English rule. It was also part of a general enclosure movement which occurred throughout Ireland and Britain at this time.

Early Modern walls

The establishment of the large colonial estates and the implementation of the 18th and 19th century acts of enclosure heralded the next major phase of wall building. No doubt considerable social disruption attended such changes. It is recorded that legal action was taken against the clergy in Kilfenora in 1712 due to their support for the local peasantry whose small holdings were being amalgamated into pasture by the cattle barons of the time. Such early modern, intact single and double-walled fields contrast with the haphazard area of small medieval enclosures of tumble walls in the vicinity of Ballykinvarga, just east of Kilfenora.

The most significant post-medieval wall-building period was between the mid 18th and the mid 19th century. Documentary evidence points to the rearrangement of the

Feidín wall, Muckinish East

small irregular fields of the lowland valleys (Ballyvaughan, for instance) into medium-sized regular fields. The many *feidín*-based walls of the coastal strip of the north Burren, typical also of south Galway, were probably built at this time. These walls are most notable in east and central Galway along the N17 and in north Clare. *Feidíns* (cobble-sized stones) cleared from the ground to protect the plough, were used as the base for the new walls. The resulting large rectangular fields (now mainly in silage) once grew grain, necessitating the distinctive layout and wall style (*balla feidín*). The north Burren was once the breadbasket of the region, presumably supplying various mills such as the Doorus tidal mill with grain. A practical benefit of the **feidín wall** is that it prevents undermining by rabbits, and it has been said anecdotally that light coming through the spaces of the larger stones startles sheep, preventing them from jumping the walls. This style of wall has been reported from Galloway in South-west Scotland and in parts of Eastern Australia where they were built, presumably by Galway emigrants after the Famine. A different style, double-built with coverstones surmounted by coping stones is found in Kentucky where they were constructed by Irish immigrants, after the Famine. To prove the point, one wall is inscribed with the name J. Kearney.
 A cameo of the work of the ambitious gentleman farmer can be seen at Northampton to the south of Kinvara. Here, the large rectangular fields averaging 2 ha are surrounded by strongly built double walls, bearing witness to the early

Buttressed Famine Relief road, Poulaphuca

Clearance pile, South Galway

Crenellated wall beside military road, New Line

Famine Relief inscribed stone, Lismorahaun

19th century amalgamation of smaller enclosures: tenant tillage bowing to landlord livestock. A number of follies – pseudo-cairns and ringforts – punctuate the otherwise featureless field system, and were obviously built from surplus stones. Such decorative use of surplus stone is to be found elsewhere in the region, often in the form of cairns, but nowhere else with such romantic effect. The switch from a largely subsistence economy to a predominantly market economy also impacted on upland areas. Many medium-sized and large upland fields enclosed mainly by single walls date from the enclosure period. However it would appear that most of the well-built double walls, enclosing large regular fields up to 8.5 ha are also contemporary. Undoubtedly many of the small, unmodified fields still identifiable on the hillsides were once 'lazy beds'. Boulder clay or glacial till 'islands' within the limestone are discernibly corrugated with old potato ridges. This is notable in the valleys of the north Burren, particularly when the sun is low. Despite having been robbed of their stones, old field boundaries also stand out. Piles of stones collected by the potato diggers to make the beds can still be seen in places. Having originally been part of the till matrix, these stones are noticeably less angular than the surface stones from the limestone itself. Apparently, evictions of cottiers from their smallholdings facilitated the enlargement of such fields. In contrast, Famine relief schemes provided employment in the form of wall and road repair and construction. Fine stonework can be seen buttressing the sides of the relief road at Rockforest. An inscription on a pillar at the side of the road near the top of the Caher valley records this relief work. An interesting section of wall, low and crenellated along its top like a linear battlement, is found along the Burren's eastern flank. It runs alongside the straight of the New Line and was apparently built by the British army, in the early 19th century, to link with Galway Bay's Martello towers: a military connection – practically and aesthetically.

Modern walls

By all accounts the wall network of the modern Burren was established by the latter part of the 19th century.
The Congested Districts Board and their successor, the Land Commission, were active in the late 19th to the early 20th centuries subdividing and reallocating former estate land. However their work seems to have impacted only in certain parts. Some subdivision of large upland holdings (>50 ha) by the Land Commission occurred in the early 20th century. However it was believed locally that hardly any new walls were built in the north Burren throughout most of the 20th century.
Since the 1980s and during Ireland's subsidy agriculture phase, substantial radical change has been wrought in parts of the Burren. This resulted in the 'reclaiming' of rough grazing land for silage, the amalgamating of small fields by removal of boundaries and in the construction of new walls. With so much emphasis on the use of machinery, few

Stone-faced concrete-block wall, South Galway

Modern machine-built wall, South Galway

walls are hand-built nowadays: many are simply stacked 'megaliths' set one on the other by the bucket of the machine. These 'weetabix' walls may be recognised not only by the size of the slabs but also by the tell-tale bucket teeth marks. Some slabs, too wide to be set on the flat are employed edgeways, in a distinctive toothed-fashion. More than a thousand hectares of the Burren, many bounded by such walls, have been modified in this manner in the last quarter of the 20th century. With the decline in subsidies in recent years, there has been less emphasis on modification of this kind. A phase of reclamation in the Ballyvaughan valley in 2005 saw a conscious return to retaining the traditional style of wall construction, even though machinery was employed. In times to come, the **machine-built wall** undoubtedly will be identified along with the **mound** or **tumble walls**, as simply another phase in the long history of wall construction in this region of walls. With more emphasis on the use of stonework in a decorative rather than functional sense, Burren residents are rediscovering the aesthetic beauty of the limestone and using it liberally in the construction of garden boundaries and house walls. Stone-facing concrete-block walls both on houses and on boundaries has become increasingly popular, creating a modern vernacular style. Most popular is a robust design of angular blocks, a metre or slightly higher. Placed in a double format, either flat or edgewise, filled with rubble or with a concrete-block core, the wall is typically concrete capped. Castellated entrance pillars – like miniature keeps – seem almost to be mandatory. While the abandonment of the structural characteristics of the raw material for the expedience of concrete is in some ways regrettable, signs of the development of an aesthetic consensus based on the appropriateness of the use of local stone is surely to be praised. It is to be hoped that the traditional use of the limestone in the construction of the drystone walls of the region will continue in the future, albeit more self-consciously than formerly.

Reclaimed land and boundary wall, Ballyallaban

A BURREN FARMER'S EXPERIENCE

The walls on my farm

Despite having spent all my life on my farm, it is only recently that I gave any thought to the walls that are on it. Walls play so many important roles in the management and everyday use of the farm that it is strange how easily they can be taken for granted. They provide shelter for livestock, protect tillage and fodder crops, provide a habitat for various types of wildlife, contribute to biodiversity – and most of all make a very effective farm boundary.

There is so much of our history in stone walls that they deserve much more attention. When our ancestors cultivated with spades, they removed the stones from the gardens piling them on top of each other to increase the space for crops, so forming our first walls. Very often these were placed between large stones that were too big to move and this accounts for the irregular shape of many of our older fields.

The walls on my farm are quite varied and have changed with each generation. The ordnance survey maps from the beginning of the last century show that there were over sixty fields in the arable part of my farm, all enclosed by stone walls. Now there is only one in the home farm and three in the outside farm.

Despite the irregular shape of the fields and poor quality of the walls, they were quite adequate, as most cultivation and harvesting were done manually. With the coming of mechanisation, my father started to enlarge the fields; building fine straight walls at least six feet high, resulting in twenty nice rectangular-shaped fields very suitable for any type of farming. These walls displayed the skills and extraordinary strength of the men who built them during the early years of the 20th century. When I switched to dairying as my main farming enterprise, all those fine walls were removed on the home farm. All that now remain are about six hundred metres on the outside farm.

The walls on the rocky parts and limestone plateau have remained as they were built hundreds of years ago – untouched except for minor repairs to comply with R.E.P.S requirements.

The walls that form the farm boundary vary greatly: some contain the remains of old dwellings, their occupants long since gone; an old limekiln is found in another part; some parts were constructed in the 1940s; others are of recent origin, built with the aid of a mechanical digger. If only walls could talk!

Michael O'Donohue, 2006

Burren Wall Timechart

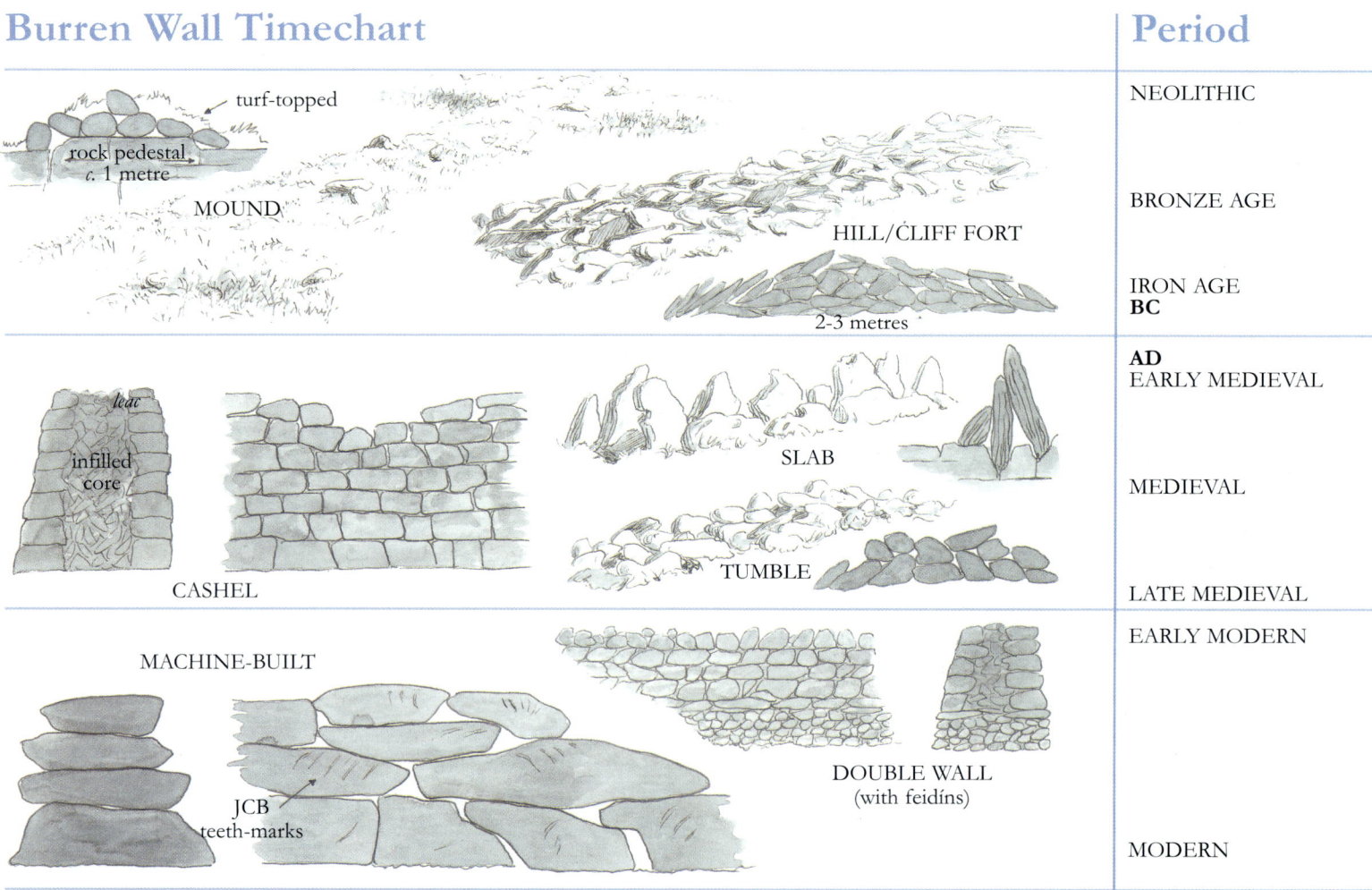

THE DRYSTONE WALL. A WORK OF SKILL, A WORK OF ART

What is it about the Burren's drystone walls that elicits such comment, such approval – even admiration? Is it the regularity of shape, the simplicity of design, the traditional mode of construction, the use of natural materials? Doubtless all of these, and more, contribute to the favourable response. In particular, as in all successful craft, the balance between function and form is both evident and pleasing: the stone wall looks 'right' in the setting of the Burren. Were the intricate network of stone on stone to be replaced by post and wire or concrete block, the effect would be so inappropriate as to be unimaginable. Not that the vulnerable landscape of the Burren has been spared the incongruous. Whether wood, iron, clay or stone, the raw material must be coaxed into use by the hands of the craftsman. Intimate knowledge of inherent traits – weight, strength, resistance to the elements, friction – define the skill of the worker and his craft. Beauty is an inevitable by-product of such endeavour.

More than five millennia of traditional construction testify to the appropriateness of the Burren wall. Though difficult

Burren road and drystone walls, Creehaun

to prove, the original Neolithic walls appear to differ little from those recently built; the same simple formula applies. It is not the failure of the wall as an entity – as enclosure, as exclosure – that has brought about change. The decline of the manual, in the face of advancing mechanical, has more to do with it. Nevertheless, even the most modern structures have the lump of limestone as the basic unit of construction.

Quarried limestone has a bright blue-grey colour: modern walls built jigsaw fashion, of angled pieces, reflect this freshness. Long-standing Burren walls on the other hand are a palette of greys and browns subtly suffusing into one another as ordained by the dominance of particular lichens and algae growing on them. Many walls are so decorated with white *Lecanora* that they have the appearance of having been rained on with whitewash: this lichen is an ubiquitous wall-topper. At the coast, however, the colouring takes the form of banding – white at the top, mustard yellow in the middle, and black at the bottom. The lichens here reflect the influence of the splash-zone and their capacity to cope with salt spray.

Style

The style of the drystone wall evokes expediency. In glacial soils or along storm beaches, where rounded stones are available, the walls are low, tiered and regular. In areas of pavement, on the other hand, the flaggy segments are stacked, horizontally or vertically, greater friction allowing greater stability – thus height. Using what is available is the consequence of ingenuity rather than conformity. In such circumstances, stubborn rock outcrops or immoveable glacial erratics may be incorporated into the wall.

Old granite or sandstone quern stones, perhaps originally

Lichen-topped wall, Finavarra

Storm beach wall, Inis Oirr

Granite erratic in wall, Finavarra

Wedge tomb incorporated into wall, Tullycommon

other eye-catching patterns result from the angular stacking of stones near or at the top of the wall. 'Herringbone' aptly describes the alternate style of stacking from course to course over the height of the wall. On the Aran Islands this loose arrangement is everywhere common. It is such a typical feature as to echo the knit-pattern of the Aran sweater. On the largest of the Islands, Tim Robinson recorded the terms *claí fidín,* translating approximately as 'fragment fence' and *clocha mháthar* 'mother stones', pillar-like uprights in the wall. On Inis Oírr, where some walls are three metres high, the pattern often loses its consistency to avail of local conditions. Where available, an upright or

fashioned from glacial erratics, find a new life in the body of some Burren walls. In places even megalithic tombs have been incorporated opportunistically by the whim of the wall-builder.

Though wall patterns tend to be different, with variation in landscape or land use, a certain rationale is evident. A striking example in old tillage country is the *feidín* base. Indeed one can trace regions of former tillage in the Burren using this patterned feature. This wall with its distinctive base-course – 'pick-ups' from ploughland – has its Irish headquarters in the flat farmland of south and central Galway, though it may also be seen in adjacent counties such as Mayo.

In the classic *balla feidín* the base courses of fist-sized stones are covered with flat horizontal stones and stacked above with more upright-orientated stones. Variations on the theme can be seen in parts of the north Burren. Some

Feidín wall with uprights, Muckinish East

27

standard (*Cloch seasaimh*) is inserted at fairly regular intervals to provide stability. The regular spacing of the uprights has spawned the phrase *brí-sa-gclaí*, a delightfully apposite reference to the strengthening function of the upright stones. In places a surfeit of uprights are jammed together, apparently unnecessarily, as though to defy the concept of pattern. These often have a function, however, doubling as gaps for cattle movement upon removal of the stones between.

Of all the features of the drystone wall, the crossing point

Aran sweater design; Fallers Sweater Shop, Galway

Eclectic style wall with uprights, Ballaghaline

or style tells us more about the mindset of the wall builders than any other. In some cases, expediency is obviously to the fore but in many, a sense of creativity, even artistry, is evident.

It is clear from the variety to be found that no blueprint exists: the style is quite simply that – an expression of style. Some of the more elegant seem poised like artworks in the structure of the wall, their function a given, their significance encapsulated in their form. One, though a mere gap in stacked uprights, is cleverly keyed into the horizontal step. Another, simply a v-shaped notch, is just the right height above the ground to admit any biped but exclude any quadruped. Yet another is carefully designed with protruding footstones on both sides. All demonstrate the inherent 'stone knowledge' of the builder, a patience born of hard physical labour, and a discernible affection for the material at hand.

These same characteristics show in the many sheep passes (*poreens* or *puickets*) to be seen in and around the Burren. Most of these undoubtedly were built during the enclosure period, when Dutton tells us there were 'immense flocks of sheep' reared in the Burren.

Coping stones, though much less distinctive than those of the north of England are common enough on strong double walls and estate boundaries.

Little effort having been made in selecting them, they top the walls with a pleasing irregularity, in keeping with most of the land they enclose.

Drystone Walls Inis Oirr

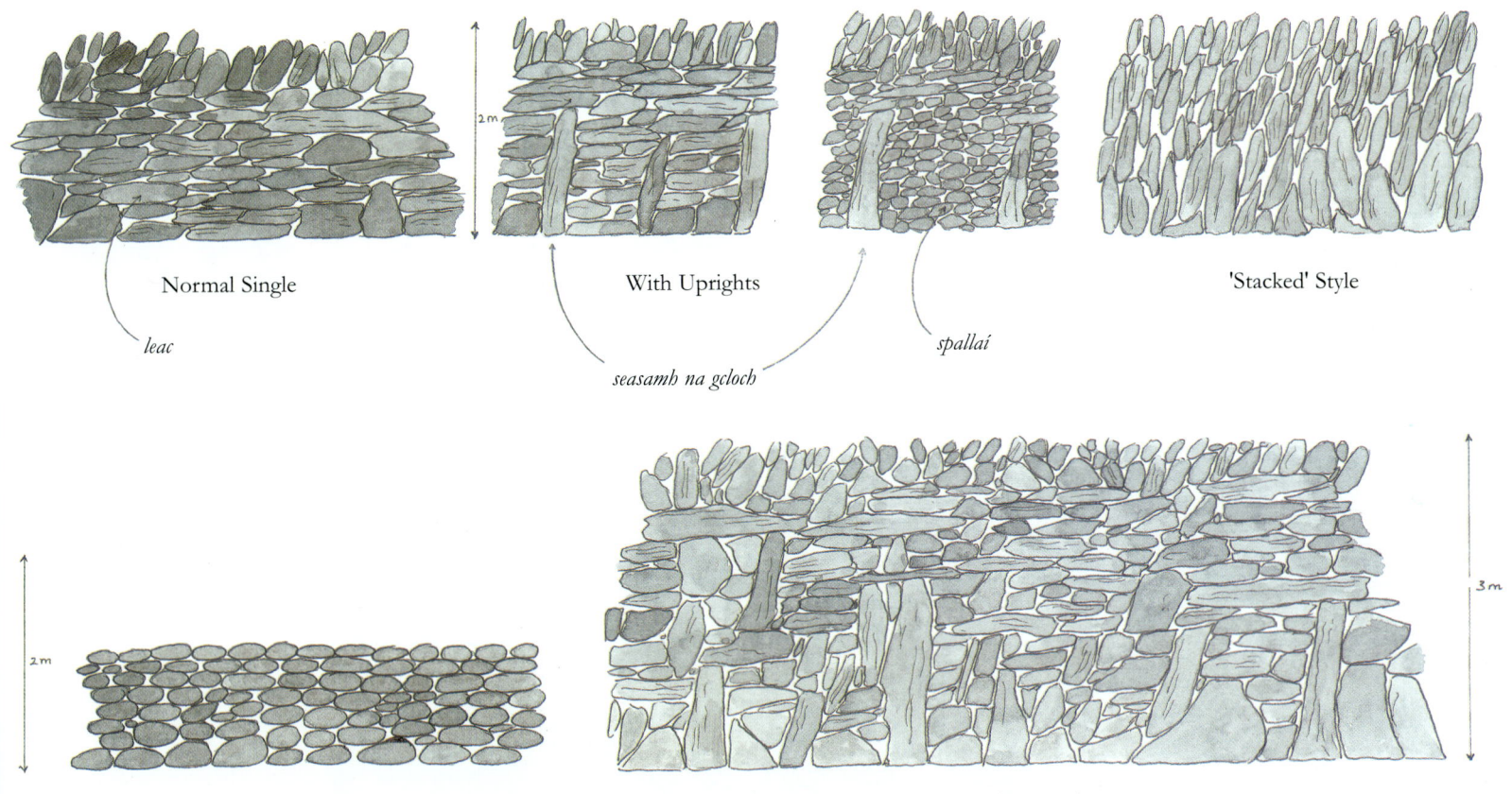

Different perspectives

A consistent feature, at least in the single walls, is light. Where it is necessary to rid the field of them, the small stones (*spallaí*) are jammed into the holes but the wind is free to blow through. In other places 'crow-stones' are left on the wall tops rather than in the gaps between the stones. The logic is simple: a perforated wall is less of a barrier to elemental forces than a solid one – therefore, in theory, more stable. This assumes, of course, that the cumulative frictional characteristic of the wall outweighs the strength of the wind. Usually it does. One is left with a strange thought: the drystone wall is not so much a case of stone on stone as stone on space: chunks of stone; chips of light. The walls thus have three discrete aesthetics: close-up, middle ground and distant. Each elicits a different response. Each has its particular magnetism.

The close experience is tactile. The hand is drawn to the sun-warmed surface, to the fossiliferous texture, to the fretted surface and the bedding planes. The stones stacked with no thought to visual conformity present the crack-lines between the bedding planes in random array.

The radical change of direction of the cracks, or their sudden truncation, seems somehow playful rather than jarring. Meanwhile the eye seeks out the 'peekaboo' holes between the stones. This is the open-plan shadowy world of overhangs and canyons, spiders' webs and snails. One is suddenly aware that with the daily cycle of the sun, the changes in the day, in the season, the circumstances for

Style with steps, Inis Oirr

Stepped style, South Galway

Stacked stone style, Clab

Sheep pass, South Galway

survival in this apparently static environment are constantly in flux. The eye re-focuses to explore the green and grey triangles beyond the wall. As often as not it will pick up the patterned aesthetic of the wall on the other side of the field. At a distance, where the individual stones lose their identity, the wall becomes a horizontal unit. The eye sweeps sideways, noting pattern – stacked, herringbone, layered, eclectic. Gate uprights, gaps or buildings, halt the ocular swivel. It is soon restarted, however for there is something compulsive, even mesmerising in planar countryside where walls dominate over other man-made structures.

Perhaps the most fascinating aesthetic is that created by distant walls. In the barren limestone country these networks take on a significance of unique proportions. From the air, the Aran Islands are reduced to a trio of jigsaw puzzles, each piece highlighted by the shadow cast by the walls. In the Burren, the threadlike boundaries stand out in stark relief in winter sunshine, giving the grey mantle of the landscape an embroidered, patchwork appearance. From the plateau top, the line of a low wall seems to meander onto the slopes, picking up rectangular and annular enclosures on the way. Losing altitude in sudden steps, its line serves to emphasise the abruptness of the limestone terraces. It is eventually lost in the hazel scrub, only to reappear as a hedgerow in the cultivated grassland of the valley. Strangest of all are the isolated stretches of wall, geometric shapes punctuating the uplands. Has the plateau become a game board for a giant's game? A more mundane explanation awaits us: sheltering for winterage cattle in harsh weather.

Horizontally and vertically stacked wall, Pullagh

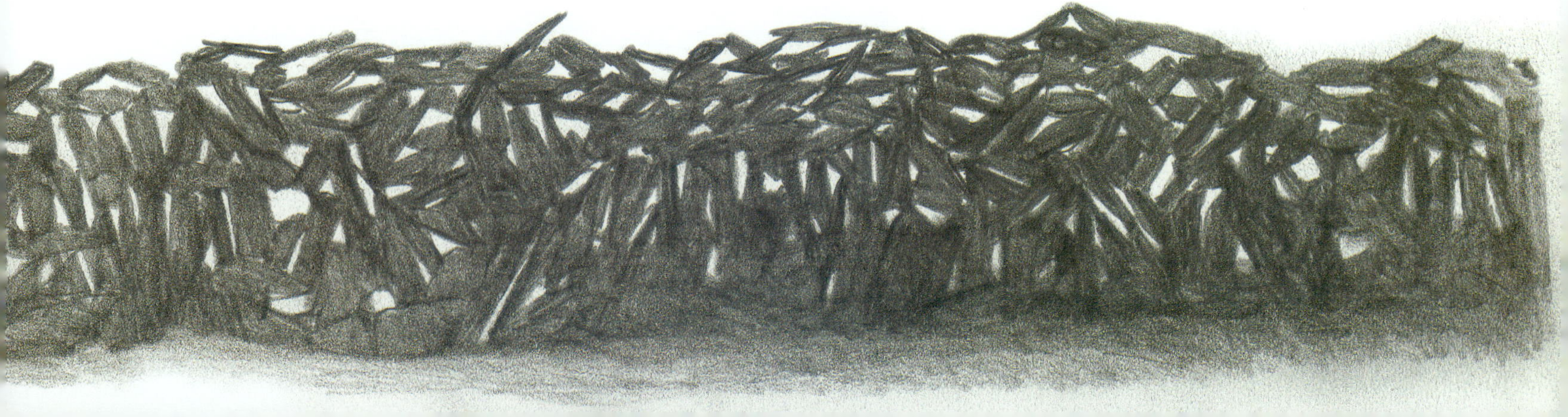

Livestock gap in stone wall, Inis Oirr

Cross-wall livestock shelter, Cappagh

VISITORS' VIEWS

'Here [in the Burren] is but one narrow road, no going out of it, and in this barony the partitions of land are made by broad stones like slate turned up edgewise.'
Dineley, 1681

'…the land was enclos'd in very large pastures with stone walls of a very singular construction. They are piled one upon another, but not flat and like the stone walls in Glocestershire, solid; but the stones are placed in such a manner, that there are interstices thro'out the whole length of the wall of about 5 or 6 inches in diameter, so that when you look upon a wall on a rising ground and see the light thro' the different vacancies, it very nearly resembles a net set in the sea to catch fish, only with this difference, that the meshes, if I may call them so, are generally triangular and not square. I wou'd defy a London mason to build one of them without serving an apprenticeship to the trade, and yet every cottager makes them in this manner. This is the only county in Ireland, or perhaps the only place in the world, where they build these kinds of nettwork walls…'
Willes, 1761

'It is moreover added to enhance the wonder that the stone walls are transparent – it is the custom of the country to

build these walls with stones that shall touch if possible only by the angles and this is said to be done under the notion that the wind passing through the intervals will not blow them down. Every field encumbered by stones which in many almost cover the surface so that it certainly is not from any want of materials.'
Woods, 1809

'While on the part of the coast of Clare that is almost entirely limestone, we hoped and believed that the excessive subdivision of the land was owing to its stony character. We saw vast heaps in the middle of little fields; and we hoped that the innumerable fences were merely a method of getting rid of the stones. But since we have come down upon a more fertile district, where there are no stones in the middle of the fields, we find the enclosures are larger.'
Martineau, 1852

'The people are literally cooking their food with dried fern, heath, brambles and branches of hazel, of which there is a scanty growth, here and there amongst the stone walls which divide field from field.'
Coulter, 1861

'These baracades [walls] are erected with no consideration for the shins of scientific explorers. It seems unfair to kick them down, as the natives do in the most reckless manner, whether crossing their own or their neighbours' lands. If you adopt the alternative of climbing which is often an operation of considerable difficulty, it is most probable that your descent will be followed by an avalanche of loose stones – still as the wall falls from you, this is safer than to kick it down in front, where there is a great risk of the stones falling towards and laming you...'
H.C.Hart, 1869

'In Clare, Galway, and in particular the Aran Islands, there are no breaks in the walls for gates, but a section of the wall is taken down and rebuilt as required. The 'gates ' are defined by pillar stones.'
Emyr Estyn Evans, 1956

'In certain areas, [on the largest of the Aran Islands]…the loose stone on offer consists of shaggy crusts or scales two or three feet across like battle-hacked shields, and the field boundaries there are scrawled in leap-frogging triangles made by leaning these shards together at capricious angles.'
Tim Robinson, 1995

'A good drystone wall knows where it stands
and what's more, it knows what it is: it belongs.
It has character and strength and it wears
Its years well: like a castle or a cathedral.'
Francis Harvey, 1996

'The walls are built on top of the rock from which time and weather split them. So no foundations are needed. Another advantage is that because of the gaps and the holes in these walls the sheep won't jump them!
Then there is the relationship of the walls to the landscape from which they seem to grow. The skill is in the positioning of each stone in relation to the others and in the sturdiness of the whole…
'Indeed colour, light and shade play upon and within the Burren's drystone walls enhancing its landscape with fine open-work, with tracery of stone and so, as Emerson says,
" The conscious stone to beauty grew."
Poyntz, 1998

'When you look around the Burren one of the first things you see are the rocks. There is such an abundance of stones here that it is no surprise that so many things are built out of them. There are castles, churches, homes, forts, walls; over 70 stone tombs in the Burren alone. More than any other stone construction I have seen more stone walls than anything else. These walls have many uses. The[y] have traditionally been used for sectioning of livestock, enclosing homesteads. According to the *Book of the Burren* there are from around 300 (Westropp) to near 450 (Tim Robinson) settlements enclosed in this manner. In today's society they are more used for sectioning off livestock than anything else. In places such as Cathair Chomáin these walls were vital to the ancient people that lived there (*Book of the Burren*, p.84).

The walls still have a high demand in modern times and still line the countryside in every direction. I was amazed at their location and construction when I first arrived in Ireland. They are very long stretching, going to the tops of many hills and are built to last. It amazes me how the walls allow wind to go through them (so as to not fall down) yet are sturdy enough not to move with the largest of gusts. I have observed several differences in the construction of stone walls throughout Ireland, and the most common feature was that they were arranged somewhat similarly using no nails, concrete or any other bonding agents. This traditional construction has definitely stood the test of time. I would say that the limestone rock of the Burren in itself is a symbol of the Burren, as are the walls. In most of the pictures that I have taken here over the duration of my stay almost all of them have stone walls somewhere in the picture. The second week we were here someone asked me, "when you think of the trip so far which is the first thing that comes to mind?" I responded, "cows and stone walls."'

Samantha Anderson, Irish Studies Student, Burren College of Art; 2004

Britain's Burren – The Yorkshire Dales

The Yorkshire Dales District of the north of England has some of the most impressive drystone wall systems of the entire U.K. Whether in Ingleborough or further south in Malham, the network of stone walls is as much a feature as the glorious landscape itself. Unlike the Burren, there is a consistent style, transcending geology (Grits, Sandstones, Limestones etc.), landscape variation, and altitude.

The drystone walls of the Scarp-region of the Dales are made from the local Carboniferous Limestone and are thus most relevant for comparison purposes.

Sheep flock, Yorkshire Dales

One important distinction, at the outset, is that of livestock. While the Burren has undoubtedly been used for other stock – even large flocks of sheep in the past – it has been traditionally a cattle-rearing region. The Yorkshire Dales, on the other hand, has traditionally been sheep country.

Historical background

Unlike the Burren, where abundant evidence remains, prehistoric wall systems are virtually absent in the Dales. At Malham, early medieval (Anglo-Saxon) field outlines may be traced but the walls themselves have been 'recycled'. 'Homestead' walls, enclosing small, irregular fields near villages are among the earliest remaining; some date from the 15th century. Some of the larger such enclosures correspond to the 16th century boom in wool production and the need to expand flocks. These show as a radial pattern of narrow, elongated fields encompassing areas of common land. Occasional ruined herders huts still found in the uplands may be contemporaneous with these developments.

The regular, rectangular network of drystone walls so characteristic of the region date from the Enclosure Acts of the late 18th century. The network as seen today was extensively in place by the mid 19th century. Most of the actual walls are therefore of the order of two hundred years old.

These walls are regarded as a national heritage and are constantly repaired both for continuing practical and

Traditional walled enclosures, Yorkshire Dales

aesthetic reasons. Master drystone wall builders are trained annually for this purpose. The methods employed have not changed in centuries.

The raw material, Carboniferous limestone and sandstone fragments removed from the 'Scars' (outcrops) by glacial scouring and deposited in the till, is collected from the immediate vicinity. Where surface littering and deposits are abundant, the process facilitates the clearing of the fields. Quarrying for material is rare. The traditional style consists of a double wall with a rubble or fragment core. The stones are graded from largest (at the bottom) to smallest (at the top). Careful selection is practiced, to the virtual exclusion of shaping and hammering.

Wall construction

A foundation is laid to a depth of about 0.10 m where possible, with an average width of about 0.75 m. A parallel row of large stones separated by a narrow layer of rubble is the usual foundation construction. The wall is then erected to a height of about 1.5m using twin rows of stone courses separated by small stones and fragments. The stones are carefully selected to maximise their characteristics and graded upwards from small boulders to handy loaf-sized cobbles at the top. The stones are always laid with their long axis horizontal.

'Throughstones', large, flat individual stones are laid at discrete heights to span from one side to the other. These provide structural grip to the wall at regular intervals. In most walls their presence is minimal though they usually protrude somewhat from the sides. In some walls, however, their presence is notable enough to form clear lines of separation. In places, one layer of throughstones is provided; in others two is normal, some 0.5m apart. Throughstones have the additional advantage of providing ledges or steps for those wishing to scale the walls, while excluding sheep from doing the same.

A row of irregularly shaped copestones (usually not used in the wall proper) are placed along the wall top. In some instances these are small and unobtrusive: in others – where sandstone is available and substituted for the usual limestone – the copestones are a distinctive feature.

Throughstones in limestone wall, Yorkshire Dales

isolated trees are subject to bark browsing, similar butt-like structures are erected. Due to their small circumference (less than 3m in diameter) these are structurally sound and pleasantly decorative.

As in the Burren, upright columns of water-worn limestone are frequently used as gateposts. In other cases large quoin-type stones are used to secure gaps and gate openings. Styles and wall-crossings vary in design from simple gaps to more elaborate, stone-sided, notch-gaps with step-stones on either side. These may even be sealed with small gates to prevent sheep using them!

Distinctive features

A structural protection is provided at a wall end. Large stones set aside for the purpose are interlocked, like quoin stones at gable/wall junctions on a stone building. This tried and tested design also ensures longevity. Where a land boundary ends, a vertical joint is evident on the wall surface.

One of the most striking features is the stylishly constructed sheep-pass – also known as a *smoot*, a *thrip*, a *cripple* or *creep* hole. This varies in size, up to about a square metre, as needs dictate. Typically, a single lintel stone spans the opening on either side of the wall. Upper layers are thus supported and secure. Smaller versions of this structure – about 0.3m – are left in places for rabbit access. These are often used as snaring points.

Gun butts for grouse shooting on the moors are also constructed in the aforementioned style. In places where

Comparing Burren walls with the walls of the Yorkshire Dales

THE BURREN	Features	THE DALES
Prehistoric to Modern	*Extant Field Systems*	Mainly Early Modern
Neolithic	*Earliest Field Systems*	Anglo-Saxon
Small-Medium	*Enclosure size*	Large
Varied	*Construction*	Consistent
Single and Double, some Feidín based,	*Traditional style*	Double, Copestones, Throughstones
Lower Carboniferous	*Geology*	Lower Carboniferous
Mixed, Corals dominant	*Fossils*	Mainly Crinoids
Common	*Chert*	Absent
Crustose lichens, Cushion mosses	*Flora*	Crustose lichens, Cushion mosses
Hare, Stoat, Wheatear, Stonechat	*Fauna*	Rabbit, Polecat, Mole, Wheatear
Cattle	*Livestock*	Sheep
Weather, Goats	*Damage*	Weather, Walkers
Wall gaps, Gates, Styles	*Passage*	Sheep-proof gates, Styles
Dearth	*Tourist Information*	Ample

Branched coral fossil in limestone

Goniatite fossil in limestone

Chert in limestone

Holes made by rock-boring shellfish

THE NATURAL HISTORY OF THE BURREN WALL

The hundreds of km of drystone walls of the Burren comprise a remarkable wildlife habitat, hosting hundreds of species of plants and animals. Most are tiny or hidden from view in the shelter of the stones but some, as highlighted here, may be easily identified, are fairly widespread and worth seeking out in the course of a ramble.

Exposure to the elements, prevailing wind direction, proximity to other habitats such as coast, woodland or wetland, and altitude, all have a bearing on the variety of species; but with some - lichens, for instance - there is remarkable consistency, reflecting the uniform nature of the rock.

The rock itself

The Burren is more or less defined by the Carboniferous limestone rock, of which the walls are comprised. There are minor irregularities such as layers of chert, occasional thin bands of sandstone and even volcanic clay (wayboards) but in general it is amazingly consistent. In places, glacial erratics of granite or occasionally sandstone are found. Such fragments, having been transported from Connemara bedrock, are sometimes found incorporated into the walls, most commonly in the northern coastal strip of the Burren. These anomalies, being acid as distinct from alkaline, support noticeably different lichens and other plants than those on limestone.

Strictly speaking, the Namurian shales, the rocks that overlay the Burren prior to the Ice Age, are not of the Burren. Thus, the walls from Lisdoonvarna south, to Doolin, the Cliffs of Moher and beyond, are not 'Burren walls'. Neither are the walls on Poulacapple and Slieve Elva (Namurian 'outliers' within the Burren) Burren walls, being acid and supporting calcifuge flora. The shale walls are visibly different, dark brown rather than grey. They are also structured differently, the regular slabs being laid horizontally, occasionally upright, and not stacked or eclectically arranged as with the limestone. Because of their regular thickness, shale slabs frequently are used as roofing material for sheds.

Fossils

The limestone walls are great places to search for fossils. The Carboniferous limestone is, in fact, composed of microscopic fossils of marine organisms. Contained within, however, are the fossils of larger, mainly extinct, creatures. Finding these shapes in the stones conjures up images of the primordial tropical sea inhabited by strange creatures, some three hundred million years ago.

Even in an area as finite as the Burren, compared with the vast Carboniferous sea, there is considerable fossil variety.

Corals, both branched and solitary kinds, are commonest along the north and west coastal districts: nothing to do with the fact that the sea nowadays washes these boundaries. The stone walls are replete with their characteristic tube-shaped fossils. Take time to look at their intricate cross-sections, like tiny spider's webs, perfectly preserved in the limestone. The corals are clear indicators that their sea was many degrees warmer than ours today.

Lamp-shells (brachiopods) are common throughout the Burren but are particularly common in the stone walls of the National Park to the south-east. They are recognisable by their white, C-shaped cross-sections. In life they resembled enormous cockles, held to the sea bed by a muscular foot or 'pod'.

Crinoids, or 'stone lilies', can indeed look like plants but their stem-like remains are fragments of structures which once supported marine animals. Crinoid fossil fragments exposed on the rock surface look strangely man-made, like bits of a necklace encased in concrete.

Other types of shellfish fossils may be found. Some, resembling periwinkles, tower-shells and oysters, apparently unchanged through eons of evolutionary time, indicate the success of certain shapes in the marine environment. Others have comprehensively disappeared; fish-fossils from the Carboniferous, for instance, are of primitive shark-like creatures or bizarre armour-plated species long gone from our oceans. Fossil corals, in section and distorted by geological processes, can look like small fish: the illusion – complete with bones and fins – can be most convincing. Cautious analysis, however, invariably reveals them as 'non-fish'. True fish fossils are rare.

Two of the most beautiful fossils are also decidedly scarce. The fossil of the **trilobite**, which resembled a giant sea slater (*Ligia*), is more likely to turn up in freshly broken limestone rather than on the weathered surface of a stone in a wall. Alive, it inhabited the limy sea bed seeking out its food with multi-cellular eyes – apparently the first creature to develop this sophisticated adaptation. Its closest present-day relative is the horseshoe crab of the eastern Atlantic, also a sea bed inhabitant which comes ashore to reproduce. The trace of the **goniatite** is a spiral, like a giant snail. This soft-bodied creature with tentacles, resembling the paper nautilus of today, fed in the open water. As with the other fossils, its soft parts quickly disappeared on death. Its hard shell, covered in the limy substrate, having ultimately turned to rock, left the traces we see today. The more familiar **ammonite**, though similar in its spiral form, was a dinosaur contemporary, inhabiting the Mesozoic oceans. In most cases the fossil replacement mineral is calcite – calcium carbonate. In some, however, it is silica. The beds and projecting lumps of **chert**, so common in the limestone, are the reconstituted remains of marine creatures such as microscopic creatures, sea urchins and other relatives, in the form of silicon dioxide. Stone Age man, unaware of the chemical nuances, avidly sought out these black glassy outcrops for the manufacture of trusty weapons and implements.

Many of the stone walls along the Burren's coastline have pockmarked stones that are full of holes. These holes are not made by fossils but rather by rock-boring creatures living in the sea today. These **piddocks** and their rock-boring mollusc relations live colonially, creating the holes as sanctuaries in the rocks on the sea bed. When subsequently they are washed up on storm beaches, the stones often end up in nearby walls.

The Finavarra peninsula has many such walls.

Lecanora *lichen*

Wall Flora

The drystone walls of the Burren support dozens of species of plants. These range from the unobtrusive lichens, algae and mosses, to showy flowers and shrubs. All exist in circumstances of significant exposure to the elements: more prolifically on the leeward, as against the windward, side; in the vertical, as distinct from the predominantly horizontal landscape. They are thus dominated by 'clingers' – sinuously rooted species that can cope with extreme conditions. Also, due to the calcareous chemistry of the wall, they are predominantly lime-lovers, or calcicoles.

Xanthoria *lichen*

Freshly quarried Carboniferous limestone is almost lustrous blue-grey. The walls, however, are dull-surfaced and tinted grey-brown, except where subject to the scouring effect of severe exposure, as on the Aran Islands. This is due mainly to the effect of endolithic lichens, encrusting and penetrating the tiny fissures in the surface, causing long-term, superficial erosion. Though found from the ground up, they are more abundant on the tops of the walls.

The most eye-catching lichens are the distinctive black, yellow and white species, occupying mainly the upper stone courses. They may be so striking as to resemble paint splashes. Clear zonation is a feature of the coast. *Verrucaria* of a number of species, and colours – black (below high tide), grey and dark brown – is widespread. The coastal species is aptly named tar lichen, since along the high-tide mark it can indeed resemble pollution. White *Aspicilia* (now *Lecanora*) lichen is commonest along the wall tops. In some places it is so bright as to define the line of the wall against the rocky grey background.

Most striking of all are the bright yellow *Xanthoria* and *Caloplaca* lichens. These vary in colour from almost greenish yellow to startlingly bright orange. They may be distinguished by examining the edge of the lichen disc: *Xanthoria* has a 'leafy' edge and can be peeled off the rock; *Caloplaca* is more like a paint stain on the rock. Like *Verrucaria* the yellow lichens form a clear zone or band along coastal walls.

Other less conspicuous species thrive in the damp declivities beneath the stones. *Collema* and *Leptogium* are examples but a hand lens and a lichenologist's handbook might be required to distinguish the particular species concerned. Prominent stones or boulders incorporated into the walls may be habitual perches for birds. Their droppings sometimes provide the nutrient enrichment to support a rich lichen flora. One bird-frequented boulder was found to have about fifty different lichens.

Many species of silicolous (as distinct from the majority, calcicolous) lichens have been identified in the Burren. In the stone walls these may be associated with the chert outcrops, the occasional pieces of Old Red and Namurian sandstone, and the granite glacial erratics, often incorporated into the walls. While the majority are crustose (like paint stains), many foliose (leafy-edged) and fruticose (tufted) species are also to be found.

Algae are contained within lichens, between microscopic layers of fungi but other surface-dwelling algae are more significant in their own right. The *Nostoc* algae, widespread in the open karst, are major agents of erosion of the limestone surface. The surface is eroded by chemical solution in a stage-by-stage process. Small surface irregularities such as those left by fossils are occupied by dried-up, wind-blown *Nostoc*; rain causes the alga to swell, to occupy the hollow, and secrete a weak humic acid. Chemical solution ensues, calcium dissolves, carbon dioxide is given off and the hollow increases fractionally in size over time. *Nostoc* erosion is a feature of the limestone country, primarily on the karst surface, but to a lesser degree on the tops of the walls.

Oedogonium or algal 'felt', from the manner in which it carpets dried up turloughs, is occasionally found draped over the walls in the base of turloughs. Grass green to begin with, it gradually bleaches white in sunlight. On the wall bases, at the edge of some turloughs, can be found a more colourful (bright orange) aerially borne alga – *Trentepohlia*. This exotic-looking alga is quite common elsewhere. It is to be seen frequently colouring the limestone parapets of bridges and other man-made habitats. It has a powdery texture and can easily be removed, unlike the yellow and orange lichens.

In the well-drained circumstances of the open limestone, mosses are naturally less significant than elsewhere in the west of Ireland. Moss-draped walls are a feature of the wet woods of Connemara. Old stone field boundaries in the dank hazel scrub of the Burren are often luxuriantly festooned with mosses and liverworts but these are considered atypical of the region in general.

Some mosses typify the calcium-rich conditions of the drystone walls. Being water dependent, they are most frequent in the saturated hollows, often near the wall base. Cushions of bright olive-coloured *Tortella* and *Breutelia* are the commonest. These, or closely related species, are also a feature of the limestone walls of the Yorkshire Dales. Walls bordering or bisecting turloughs have an especially distinctive pair of associated mosses. The dark brown (black at a distance) *Cinclidotus* marks the normal upper limit of flooding of the turlough. Even when dry, or from the air, the fringe of black moss stands out, like a dirty bath-stain. Though physically more robust *Fontinalis* (rope-moss), a dark green species is less tolerant of aerial exposure.

It grows at a lower level than the *Cinclidotus*, on stones etc. closer to the turlough swallow hole. This zonation has its parallel in the seaweed succession of the intertidal zone. Both mosses grow in such abundance as to completely cover the stones of the wall and to exclude the growth of other species.

Trentepohlia alga on stone wall

Dry turlough, South Galway

Ferns are common and noticeable plants of the stone walls, especially the denser packed double walls. Smaller calcicolous species dominate. Perhaps the most recognisable, from its strap-like fronds, is hart's tongue fern (*Phyllitis scolopendrium*). In places this elegant species with its 'herringbone' spore arrangement emerges from every nook and cranny on the ground and protrudes from the sides of the walls. The beautiful and rare maidenhair fern (*Adiantum capillus-veneris*) is not normally found in the walls, favouring unlit wet crevices and cave entrances, but its relative, maidenhair spleenwort (*Asplenium trichomanes*) is a common incumbent. Both have wiry black stems while the spleenwort has a distinctive ladder-like structure. Black spleenwort (*Asplenium adiantum-nigrum*), also black-stemmed but with a triangular form overall, is less common. Wall-rue (*Asplenium ruta-muraria*) our tiniest species, looking more like a garnish of parsley than a fern, adorns old loosely mortared walls in preference to dry, stone-built, examples. Identification may be quickly established by checking for the black spores on the back of the fronds.

The two finest ferns of the stone walls are surely the rusty-back (*Ceterach officinarum*) and the polypody (*Polypodium australe*). Both are commoner in the stronger, double walls. The rusty-back, true to its name, is covered on its back with red-brown scales, hiding the spore structures. It is the quintessential Burren fern, being capable, more so than the others, of coping with the extreme conditions of wetness and drought. Botanist Charles Nelson has described them as follows: 'Rusty-back can form a dense capping on walls and on shattered pavement is abundant even when other plants are absent…Its singular capacity to flourish through sodden winters and scorching summers allows it to colonise even the walls of the green roads.' Polypody, bright green with a most distinctive alternate arrangement of the pinnae (frond segments), sports twin rows of orange spore capsules on the reverse. Both rusty-back and polypody appear early in the season as tightly furled 'crosiers'. Rusty-back reverts to this form during periods of drought. Other species such as brittle bladder fern (*Cystopteris fragilis*) can occasionally be found on the walls but they are not typical of the habitat. Like the black spleenwort it may have dark stems but the pinnae are neater-looking, more like little oak-leaves.

Ferns and mosses on stone wall

Flowers

Certain species of flowers are characteristic of the walls. The same select suite may be encountered again and again throughout the Burren. Plunkett-Dillon, in describing the tumble walls of the Burren, refers to many being overgrown with mosses and herbs such as thyme, lady's mantle, glaucous sedge and sheep's fescue. Indeed the *condition* of the wall has a bearing on the predominant plants found thereon. Because walls are changeable, marginal habitats, often subject to exposure, opportunistic plants do well. Two of the most typical are the tiny, white-flowered, rue-leaved saxifrage (*Saxifraga tridactylites*) and the little pink geranium, herb Robert (*Geranium robertianum*). The former flowers early, often in March, and may be regarded as the harbinger of the Burren's entire flowering season. It occupies small crevices and solution hollows on the tops of the walls and with its red stems and leaf rosette adds a little colour to the grey background. Here it may be joined by another tiny, white-flowered annual – whitlow grass (*Erophila verna*), which resembles the saxifrage but lacks the former's indented leaves. Herb Robert may blossom at any time throughout the year. Indeed it can often be found in flower in the heart of the winter. It grows mainly in the bases or sides of walls where its pink flowers and red and green (musk-smelling) leaves catch the eye.

In places of shade, on roadsides or in the hazel scrub, a suite of flowers may occur at the base of the wall, particularly in spring. Typical examples are dog violet (*Viola riviniana*), wood sorrel (*Oxalis acetosella*), barren strawberry (*Potentilla sterilis*), lesser celandine (*Ranunculus ficaria*). Despite their association with walls, they are primarily concerned with the shade provided and cannot be described as wall-plants – unlike the various stonecrops. Two species are common: biting stonecrop (*Sedum acre*) and the introduced or escaped garden plant, white stonecrop (*Sedum album*). These succulents have fleshy pink leaves designed to deal with drought and desiccation, and yellow or white, star-shaped flowers. They are as much at home on walls as on the limestone pavement.

Mossy saxifrage on ramparts, Cahercommaun

Two beautiful white flowers, characteristic of the tumble walls of the Burren's cashels and medieval field boundaries, are mossy saxifrage (*Saxifraga hypnoides*) and field mouse-ear (*Cerastium arvense*). The former forms mossy cushions over the stonework, often providing circumstances for the latter to thrive. At Cahercommaun cliff-fort both cover entire sections of the collapsed ramparts.

Three less conspicuous plants are typical of the masonry of the ruined towerhouses and ecclesiastical structures. Navelwort (*Umbilicus rupestris*), ivy-leaved toadflax (*Cymbalaria muralis*), and the well-named pellitory-of-the-wall (*Parietaria diffusa*) may be found individually or in places together in such habitats. Navelwort, so named due to the navel-like dimple in the round leaf, grows abundantly on Corcomroe Abbey. The small but pretty purple and white flowers of toadflax are occasionally found on roadside walls and on bridge parapets. Pellitory is more confined to lime-mortar interstices where it often grows, also in structures comprised of acid rock.

It is hard to believe that wall lettuce (*Mycelis muralis*), now found throughout the Burren, was unrecorded there until the 1930s. Its fine crimson stems topped by small lemon-yellow flowers today seem to occur everywhere in the grikes and, less frequently, despite its name, in walls. Fairy foxglove (*Erinus alpinus*) is also a newcomer, actually a garden escape, being found in the lime mortar and limestone fissures of the Pinnacle well folly on the Blackhead road and at one or two other Burren locations.

One plant, ivy (*Hedera helix*), grows in walls throughout the region. A woodland species typically creeping up trees, it has adapted to the open landscape sending its sinuous stems horizontally along the grikes and interweaving itself through numerous walls. In its early stages it can consolidate the wall but later, as its roots and stems thicken, it dislodges stones and ultimately causes collapse much to the annoyance of local farmers. For this reason it is regularly grubbed up and destroyed by them.

Whitethorn in blossom, Mullaghmore

Blackberries

Certain shrubs are synonymous with the walls. Hazel (*Corylus avellana*), a most ubiquitous shrub of the Burren, is a notorious wrecker of drystone walls. In its coppiced form it grows multi-stemmed through and across old walls causing their eventual collapse. Blackthorn (*Prunus spinosa*), a common hedge plant of the Burren, also grows in the walls but is less destructive than the hazel. Its 'candy-floss' white blossom magically adorns the field boundaries each April. Its foliage is an important refuge for innumerable insects and higher animals. Whitethorn's (*Crataegus monogyna*) aromatic blossom is May's gift to the Burren's boundaries. Little damage is associated with the shrub, and its berries provide an important food supply for birds in winter. Its isolated and bent-over profile, a consequence both of the effects of wind and sea salt, adds character to the otherwise stark and treeless uplands. Other less common blossoming and fruiting shrubs found in association with walls include spindle (*Euonymus europaeus*), guelder rose (*Viburnum opulus*), crab apple (*Malus sylvestris*), dog rose (*Rosa canina*) and buckthorn (*Rhamnus catharticus*). These former elements of the woodland shrub-layer are nowadays components of the linear woodland of the hedgerows. They often occur in a semi-prostrate form along the more exposed wall boundaries.

In the absence of tracts of mixed woodland in the open Burren, the floristically diverse walls and hedgerows provide a welcome refuge for equally diverse fauna.

Fauna

At a glance the wall is a lifeless place, too exposed, too devoid of cover to support wildlife. A drive by, even a steady walk alongside a wall tends to reinforce this misconception. If one takes the time to look closely at the stones themselves, or better, in the shadows between them, another world is revealed. It is neither the sunny, showy world of the meadow nor the fleeting, glimpsed world of the open limestone but a furtive, sedentary one of gaps and crevices, of undisturbed torpidity and sudden exposure. Turn over a sizable stone, not at the top, but near the base or on the ground beside the wall, and see the life revealed.

Orb-web spider

Woodlouse spider

Invertebrates

The wall is the habitat for a wide range of mini-beasts, most of which are so small or so unobtrusive as to be largely ignored. These include springtails, nematode worms, and others almost invisible to the eye. Velvet mites are also tiny, but in their wanderings stand out vividly red against the grey limestone. Bristletails, segmented mini-beasts with spiny tails, are clearly visible. They and woodlice, defying the limitations of their name, are commonly to be found feeding on organic morsels beneath the stones. The grey

Snails: Glass snails; Garden snail; Banded snail; Door snails

51

Wall brown butterfly

woodlice with their segmented bodies are in fact isopod crustaceans: as they scurry to the damp recesses like miniature trilobites, they give a clue to their ancient, marine origins. The silvery-bodied bristletails suggest similar origins but three pairs of legs reveal them as wingless insects. These, and other detritus-feeders, are hunted by centipedes and spiders. A formidable spider – *Dysdera* – specialises in hunting woodlice. Its sharp jaws can be clearly seen at close range. However, due to its nocturnal habits it is not often noticed. One often comes across the beautiful silken retreat of *Segestria*, a related species, its interior full of tiny tan-coloured spiderlings. Tube-web and tiny jumping spiders are also common inhabitants of the stone walls. The most obvious, however, are the large orb-web spiders, (*Araneus diadematus*) which, particularly in autumn, festoon the shadowy gaps with their elaborate webs. They are striking, positioned in the middle of the web, their fat abdomen marked with a silver cross. Harvestmen with their tiny bodies and eight long, spindly legs, often seen on the tops of the walls, are not true spiders and not strictly predatory. With such an availability of calcium with which to fashion their shells, snails are much commoner than slugs. Like miniature livestock, they graze the lichens and mosses and retreat to the shadows in times of drought. The tiny grey spire of the door snail (*Clausilia*), though commonplace, is not often seen on the surface. The dowdy glass snail (*Oxychilus*) and its flamboyantly striped relative, (*Cepaea*), are commonly encountered on the wall exterior. The large brown garden snail (*Helix aspersa*) shuns bright sunlight. Their shells, often found in dozens at the bases of walls, have spawned 'snail graveyard' folklore.

The most striking of the wall invertebrates are the butterflies and moths. Many species in transit or disturbed from adjacent grassland or emerging with the cycle of the day, or season, will settle temporarily on the uppermost stones. A few, however, are so dependent as to be synonymous with the stone wall. The wall brown butterfly (*Lasiommata mergera*), true to its name, is often seen sun-bathing on the warm stones. Bright orange-tan in colour, it often settles close to patches of lichen, apparently for camouflage. The grayling (*Hipparchia semele*) relies on the camouflage of its mottled underwings as protection when basking on the wall. It will readily adjust its position so as not to cast a tell-tale shadow on the surface. Some moths, notably the grey dagger (*Acronicta psi*), so resemble the limestone in their cryptic pattern that they may remain utterly undetected until forced to move by an inadvertently placed hand. Others such as the gorgeous burnet and cinnabar moths will perch with impunity on the tops of the walls. Their red and black colour – warning of the poisons in their body fluids – is a sufficient deterrent to would-be predators. Certain butterflies, moths and bees may be found occasionally hibernating in the interstices of a double wall, though they usually prefer the security of the masonry of an old ruin. Occasionally also a suspended pupa is uncovered in the dark innermost confines.

Lizard and grasshopper

Hibernating newts

Vertebrates

Newts are common inhabitants of turloughs, spending several months of their summer aquatic stage beneath the surface of the retreating waters. From October onwards they seek drier circumstances for hibernation. In winter they can be found often only metres away from the high-water mark beneath the basal stones of walls. Sometimes dozens can be found together, curled up like miniature rubber lizards, in recesses beneath the stones. In the warmth of the hand they squirm and come out of their torpidity. This practice is not recommended, however, as it interferes with their natural seasonal cycle.

The frog (*Rana temporaria*) will sometimes hop out of a wall but hibernation is normally practiced in wetter places. Our lizard (*Lacerta vivipara*) also hibernates but not normally under the stones of a wall. Indeed, it shuns water, preferring well-drained sandy or rocky places. Unlike the newt, it basks in and is energised by sunlight. It is most likely to be seen on hot summer days, near the top, on the downwind side of the wall. Its movements are so fast, however, that one is often left doubting one's eyes after a chance encounter. Sometimes several may be seen together on a short, sheltered length of a drystone wall. They are thus vulnerable to predators, such as kestrels, from above, or stoats, from below. Lizards slough their skins in moult, and the fine translucent skin may be found discarded at the bottom of a wall, often in a sunny place.

Birds

Birds of many species use walls as perches. High points, prominent boulders in the wall and stone gateposts are particularly favoured: they are usually abundantly marked by droppings. This nutrient enrichment gives rise to rich lichen growth – yellow and white crustose and foliose lichens are typical. Commonly associated birds are meadow pipits (*Anthus pratensis*), pied wagtails (*Motacilla alba*), stonechats (*Saxicola torquata*), wheatears (*Oenanthe oenanthe*), mistle thrushes (*Turdus viscivorous*), hooded crows (*Corvus corone*), wood pigeons (*Columba palumbus*) and cuckoos (*Cuculus canorus*). The cuckoo, less common in Ireland than formerly, is still well represented in the Burren. It is not unusual to hear six or more calling from different parts on a summer morning. Cuckoos clearly use the stone walls both as song perches and viewing posts from which to spot potential foster parents for their offspring. Meadow pipits appear to be their most usual victims in the Burren. The dunnock (*Prunella modularis*) and the robin (*Erithacus rubecula*) will occasionally abandon cover to hunt for invertebrate food in the wall but the wren (*Troglodytes troglodytes*) is the quintessential drystone wall bird. Whether at the seaside or on the top of the plateau, the wren can be expected to show itself in the wall. Indeed, its status as one of our commonest Irish birds is owed to its capacity to occupy and spread throughout the length and breadth of the country along the boundary network. The wall provides the wren with all its necessities: a song post; shelter from the vagaries

Meadow Pipit display flight

Cuckoo with pipit's egg

Stonechat

of the elements; abundant food in the form of insect larvae, spiders, mites and a host of other invertebrates; a secure structure in which to build its mossy nest; and a quick escape route for a creature which prefers hopping to flying. Birds of prey perching on walls may deposit pellets on the topmost stones or on the ground nearby. Pellets, 'packages' of undigested organic material – mainly fur, feathers and bones – are highly recognisable as to species. Long-eared owl (*Asio otus*) pellets, for instance, are usually about 4 cm long, cylindrical in shape and full of the greyish fur and bones of rodents. Barn owls (*Tyto alba*), on the other hand, deposit shiny black pellets. Though seldom seen, both birds reside in the Burren. The barn owl is much scarcer. Kestrels also create pellets. These are invariably smaller and often full of beetle cases, besides fur and bones.

The sparrowhawk (*Accipter nisus*) regularly uses the stone wall as a shield while hunting. By flying low along one side and flipping suddenly over to the other, it ambushes unsuspecting ground-feeding birds.

Wren on moss-covered wall

Long-eared owl pellet

Wheatear

Mammals

Many of the Burren's mammals utilise the stone walls. They provide cover both for the delightful field mouse (*Apodemus sylvaticus*) and the not so delightful brown rat (*Rattus norvegicus*); the latter mainly near human habitation. James Fairley's trapping programme showed that the seldom-seen field mouse is in fact surprisingly abundant in the Burren. This is born out by the caches of hazelnuts frequently to be found in the gaps between stones at wall bases. The nuts, typically opened at one end (as distinct from those typically split by the squirrel), reveal themselves where walls have collapsed or are being rebuilt. Quiet, persistent, squeaking emanating from the base of a stone wall may well be that of the pigmy shrew (*Sorex minutus*). Patient observation is sometimes rewarded with a close view of a 'caravan' of these little beasts on their way to who knows where. The hedgehog (*Erinacus europaeus*), strangely scarce in the Burren, is not a typical wall creature. Bats, which regularly patrol stone walls for insect prey at dusk, will occasionally settle to pick off an unsuspecting moth. They have even been seen retreating into the wall to feed on air-caught prey. Recent investigation has shown the Burren to be especially well-endowed with bats, nine of the ten Irish species having been identified there. Many hibernate in souterrains and caves.

The commonest large mammal in the Burren is the hare (*Lepus timidus hibernicus*). An open country creature, the sprightly hare will not be contained by the Burren's walls.

Stoat

One disturbed at the roadside will run a short distance along the road before leaping even the highest of the walls. Not so the rabbit (*Oryctolagus cuniculus*): Its frenetic zig-zag usually ends with a scurry into a hole or a gap.
Though locally abundant, it is much less widespread in the Burren than its larger relative.
The fox (*Vulpes vulpes*) is closely associated with the walls. Flattened grass tracks along the bases of many show the limits of fox territories; these often converge to meet at a low point or gap in the wall. Foxes are also consummate leapers: they will hop to the top of a stone wall without disturbing a stone or making a sound.
The heftier badger (*Meles meles*), which also makes evening rounds of the wall bases, looks for low points over which it can scramble, its long claws leaving tell-tale scratches on the stones. Foxes and badgers will also leave clearly-recognisable droppings on or near crossing points to

emphasise their boundaries to others of the species. Pine martens (*Martes Martes*) will do the same. The dropping of the pine marten is highly recognisable: black, spirally formed, with seed or beetle cases, it is often deposited in a prominent position on top of a stone wall. Such traces are commonly found where the wall is in or near the hazel scrub: the creature itself is much less frequently seen. The stoat (*Mustela ermina*) is surely *the* wall mammal of the Burren. A view of one dancing along the top of a wall, in the course of a walk or from the car window, is an unexpected thrill for many visitors. The antics of the little animal are so swift, so athletic as to stop people in their tracks. Equally so for the curious stoat, allowing magically intimate views. Stoats, of course, are not out to entertain. They have a more grisly agenda, the wall providing both hunting ground and observatory for prey. The stoat feeds on a wide range of prey, from birds and their chicks to small fish in rock pools.

The feral goat (*Capra hircus*) is also intimately connected with the Burren's walls, though at least in the eyes of the farmers, in a less benign way than the other mammalian inhabitants. The herds of goats, progeny of former domestic animals, roam the uplands feeding on the grassy reserves. In moving from one grazing area to another they may pour through a gap, dislodging stones or causing general collapse of a section of wall. In the past, when repairing walls was part of the annual regimen of the herders, enclosures could be readily restored. Nowadays, with declining personnel and less emphasis on manual labour, such remedial work is difficult to sustain. The goat has thus become the *bête noire* of many livestock farmers in the Burren, and its burgeoning herds are culled from time to time. Paradoxically, the Burren needs a grazer/browser like the goat to help control the spread of hazel scrub, which threatens to engulf whole tracts of the region. In the past, the native red deer (*Cervus elaphus*) would have fulfilled this function. Perhaps the time is right to consider reintroducing the deer for this, and other reasons. It would, of course, be impossible to contain them with the existing wall system; deer fencing, over a wide area, would be prohibitively expensive. One can only speculate on the impact that reintroduction might have in the long-term. It seems likely, however, that the more delicate deer would be less destructive than its feral counterpart.

Badger scratch marks

STONE WALLS WORKPACK

STONE WALL CODE FOR NATURE DETECTIVES

Do not lean against the wall when examining it

Do not remove stones from the wall

If a stone is lifted to look for mini-beasts, be sure to replace it

This attractive workpack has been designed particularly for national schools as participatory material for both teachers and pupils. It may also be used by families who would like to learn, in a unique way, about a familiar, though often overlooked, aspect of our countryside. Though designed with the limestone walls of the west of Ireland in mind, the theme and the pack, with slight modifications to take account of local conditions, may be utilised in any part of the country.

Using the workpack children are encouraged to become **nature detectives**; to become aware of, to explore and look closely at, the various distinctive characteristics of drystone walls in their locality. They are encouraged to seek out features such as fossils, erratics, badger scratch-marks etc. and to take note of the various flora and fauna found living in the wall. Naturally safety is to the fore and a **stone wall code** emphasises care and respect for the wall itself and its various inhabitants.

Fun indoor activities are outlined in the workpack: **build your own stone wall** – lifesize, with cardboard cut-outs, to be stuck on to the school corridor wall; or in miniature, with playdo or plasticine, showing field layouts and different wall styles.

The workpack includes a full colour, A2-sized **poster** depicting the drystone wall with its typical flora and fauna. Though the setting is that of the limestone country of the west of Ireland, many of the species are found in similar drystone walls, elsewhere in the country. As a class lesson children are encouraged to illustrate their own section of wall, drawing on the various species found in fieldwork. A **jig-saw** of the poster, aimed mainly at younger children, is included in the workpack.

This workpack can be ordered from ENFO, at 17 St. Andrew Street, Dublin 2. Ph.(01)8883925, email brendankeenan@environ.ie

National Schoolchildren

Bibliography

Aalen F.H.A., Whelan Kevin & Stout, Mathew;1997. *Atlas of the Irish Rural Landscape,* Cork University Press

Clinton M.; 2001. *The Souterrains of Ireland*, Wordwell Publishing, Co. Wicklow

Cunningham G. (1978, '80, '92); *Burren Journey, B.J. West, B.J. North,* Shannonside Tourism, & Burren Research Press, Ballyvaughan, Clare

D'Arcy G. & Hayward J.; 1992. *The Natural History of the Burren,* Immel Publishing, U.K.

Dunford B.; 2002. *Farming and the Burren,* Teagasc, Dublin

Dutton H.; 1808. *Statistical Survey of County Clare,* Royal Dublin Society, Dublin

Evans Emyr Estyn; 1996. *Ireland and the Atlantic Heritage,* The Lilliput Press, Dublin

Garner L.; 1984. *Drystone Walls,* Shire Publications Ltd. U.K.

Harvey F.; 1996. *Stone, The Boa Island Janus*, Dedalus Press,

Jones C.; 2004. *The Burren and the Aran Islands, Exploring the Archaeology,* Collins Press, Cork

McAfee P.; 1997. *Irish Stone Walls,* O'Brien Press, Dublin

McCarthy P.M. & Mitchell M.E.; 1988. *Lichens of the Burren Hills & the Aran Islands,* Officina Typographica, Galway

Ó Céirín C.; 1998. *The Outlandish World of the Burren,* Rathbane Publishing, Co. Clare

Ó Dálaigh B. (Ed);1998. *The Stranger's Gaze; Travels in County Clare (1534- 1950),* Clasp Press, Ennis, Co. Clare

Plunkett Dillon E.; 1985-86. *The Field Boundaries of the Burren, Co. Clare,* Ph.D. Thesis, T.C. Dublin

Poyntz S.; 2000. *A Burren Journal,* Tír Eolas, Kinvara, Co Galway

Preston C.D., Pearman D.A., Dines T.D.; 2002. *New Atlas of the British & Irish Flora,* Oxford University Press, U.K.

Robinson T. *Stones of Aran,* (1986); Pt. 1, *Pilgrimage,* (1995); Pt.2, *Labyrinth;* Liliput Press, Dublin & Penguin, London

Rowney E.; 1996. *Drystone Wall Features,* Matthew Ward Rowney Publ. U.K.

Simms M.; 2001. *Exploring the Limestone Landscapes of the Burren and the Gort Lowlands,* published by burren karst.com

Swinfen A.; 1992. *Forgotten Stones,* The Lilliput Press, Dublin

Tír Eolas; 1991. *The Book of the Burren,* Tír Eolas, Kinvara, Co Galway

Tír Eolas; 1994. *The Book of Aran,* Tír Eolas, Kinvara, Co Galway

Westropp T.J.; 1999. *Archaeology of the Burren, Prehistoric Forts and Dolmens in North Clare,* Clasp Press, Ennis, Co. Clare

Wotring J.; 2003. *Drystone Walls of Kentucky and the Irish Connection,* Unpublished study, U.S.

Yorkshire Dales National Parks Authority; 2000. *Nature in the Dales: Limestone Pavement,* YDNPA, U.K.

Acknowledgements

I would like to thank the following organisations which in one way or another helped to bring this project into being. Special thanks to Clare Heritage Forum and Clare County Council for their encouragement. Financial assistance was received from Clare County Council (Arts funding), and from the Leader Rural Development Programme. The author is grateful as well to Galway County Council; Burren Beo; Burren College of Art; Ennis Library; Trinity College Library; Clare Museum; glór, Ennis; Tír Eolas; Teagasc; Yorkshire Dales National Parks Authority.

I received help from numerous individuals including: Congella McGuire; Sinéad Cahill, Gerard Kennedy; Keeran Kennedy; Paul Gosling; Marguerita Heffernan; Anne Korff; Brendan Dunford; Caoilte Breatnach, Michael O'Donohue; Marie Mannion; Kate Hilditch; Robert Ellis; Marcus Collier; Andrew Brown-Jackson; Patrick McAfee; Martin Feely; Seamus Caulfield; Michael Gibbons; Eoin O'Sullivan; Andrew Melia; Maurice O'Keefe; Tomás Conneely; Breandán Ó Madagáin; Jonathan Wotring.

Tír Eolas is an independent publishing house based in Doorus near Kinvara, Co. Galway. The name, **Tír Eolas**, can be translated as "knowledge of the land". **Tír Eolas** prides itself on producing books, guides and maps that combine text and illustration to an exceptionally high standard providing information on Irish history, archaeology, landscape, culture and tradition.

Tír Eolas has published seven **Guides and Maps**, covering the Burren, South Galway, Kinvara, Medieval Galway and Loch Corrib. They give detailed information on the archaeological and historical sites, the birds, animals and flowers to be seen and the natural features found in the area covered by each map. They are the ideal aid to the discovery and exploration of the Burren and South Galway.

Tír Eolas Guides and Maps
The Burren Series:
Ballyvaughan, Kilfenora, O'Brien Country
also available as a pack
Medieval Galway
Corrib Country
Kinvara, Kiltartan

Tír Eolas Books
Alive, Alive-O, the shellfish and shellfisheries of Ireland, by Noël P. Wilkins, 2004.
Drawing on mythology, archaeology, history, oral tradition, biology, economics and a wealth of personal experience, this book tells the story of Ireland's shellfish and shellfisheries.
ISBN 1-873821-20-4 PB

The Shores of Connemara, by Séamus Mac an Iomaire, translated by Pádraic de Bhaldraithe, 2000.
A naturalist's guide to the seashore and coastal waters of Connemara, Co. Galway and an account of the life of the people who lived there in the late nineteenth and early twentieth century. ISBN 1-873821-14-X PB

A Burren Journal, by Sarah Poyntz, 2000.
Sarah Poyntz's diaries give a striking picture of life in the unique landscape of the Burren. She describes the changing seasons, the birds and animals, the wild flowers for which the Burren is famous and the lives of the people of the village of Ballyvaughan. The illustrations by Anne Korff and Gordon D'Arcy bring her words to life. ISBN 1-873821-13-1 PB

The Book of the Burren, edited by Jeff O'Connell and Anne Korff, 1991.
An introduction to the geology, natural history, archaeology and history of the Burren region. 2nd edition 2002.
ISBN 1-873821-15-8 PB

The Book of Aran, edited by John Waddell, Jeff O'Connell and Anne Korff, 1994.
An introduction to the natural history, archaeology, history, folklore and literary heritage of the Aran Islands.
ISBN 1-873821-03-4 PB

Kinvara, a Seaport Town on Galway Bay, written by Caoilte Breatnach and compiled by Anne Korff, 1997.
Social history and folklore seen through photographs.
ISBN 1-873821-07-7 PB

Women of Ireland, by Kit and Cyril Ó Céirín, 1996.
A biographical dictionary of Irish women from earliest times to the present. It documents the rich and varied contributions women have made to the shaping of Irish history and culture.
ISBN 1-873821-06-9 PB

The Shannon Floodlands, by Stephen Heery, 1993.
A natural history of the callows, the distinctive landscape seasonally flooded by the River Shannon.
ISBN 1-873821-02-6 PB

Not a Word of a Lie, by Bridie Quinn-Conroy, 1993.
A portrait of growing up in a small community in the West of Ireland.
ISBN 1-873821-01-8 PB

For further information,
Tír Eolas
Newtownlynch, Doorus, Kinvara, Co. Galway.
Tel/Fax: 091 637452.
e-mail: info@tireolas.com
Order on-line: www.tireolas.com